Called to Write
Chosen to Publish
inspiration for Christian writers

Matthew 22:14
"For many are called, but few are chosen."

Published by
OUR WRITTEN LIVES, LLC

Our Written Lives provides publishing services to authors in various educational, religious, and human service organizations. For information, visit www.OurWrittenLives.com.

Copyright ©2015 Rachael Hartman
Updated 2018

Library of Congress Cataloging-in-Publication Data
Hartman, Rachael 1983
Called to Write, Chosen to Publish

Library of Congress Control Number: 2015915068
ISBN: 978-1-942923-10-7 (paperback)

Unless otherwise noted, Scriptures are from the King James Version, public domain. Alternate versions used are noted, and belong to the copyright holders thereof.

Called to Write Chosen to Publish
inspiration for Christian writers

by Rachael Kathleen Hartman

Dedication

For Jesus . . .
The Lord of my Life,
the One who called me by His grace.
I will dwell in the House of the Lord forever.

For my family . . .
I love you with all of my heart.
Thank you for always supporting me.
I will always be here for you.

For all of the authors and writers I have had the pleasure
to work with, and will have the pleasure to work with . . .
Thank you for believing in me and trusting me with
your books. I'm honored God brought us together to
produce books to bless the world and His Kingdom.

For every person who desires to be an author or feels
the call to write, and for those who simply love to write . . .
Thank you for reading my book.
I pray God blesses and inspires you.

Contents

Introduction	9
Called to Write	11
Out of His Treasure	13
My Call to Write & Publish	17
Known and Read	23
A Legacy of Words	25
A Good Matter	27
Spirit-Led Writing	29
Writing From My Heart	31
Who is Leading?	33
Writing to Heal	39
Healed Enough to Publish	43
To the Chief Musician	47
A Good Scribe	51
The Man with the Inkhorn	55
The Truthful Pen	61
Scribes and Pharisees	63
Writing with Grace	69
And, Behold, It Was Very Good	73
The Making of Many Books	75
The Author & Finisher of Our Faith	79
Scriptures for Writers	81
Scripture Resources	93
About the Author	103

Introduction

This small book of inspirational thoughts comes from the many times I've prayed for wisdom throughout my writing journey. I thank God for His Spirit and Word speaking to my heart and leading me along the way.

Some of the ideas I share are shorter; others are longer. Some include my personal journey into writing and publishing, and others focus on lessons I've learned along the way. I hope what I've recorded can help you as you write and publish.

I've prayed for each reader—that the Lord would speak to your heart as you read. I've prayed you would take what benefits you and leave what does not. And that you would find the strength to stay committed to write, and to persevere through the publishing process.

You *can* make a difference in the Kingdom of God through the writing and publishing ministry. I pray the Lord leads you, opens doors and closes doors, and blesses you personally as you write for Him.

Rachael Hartman

Called to Write

Matthew 23:34
"... Behold, I send unto you prophets, and wise men, and scribes ..."

What has God called you to write? What treasure has He developed within you? What have you faced and overcome in your life? What have you learned that can help others?

Your answers to these questions will shape the vision and focus of your writing.

Something about your book will capture your readers' attention. It's the same way your personality may open the door to a conversation and eventually allow you to share the Gospel with someone new. You may or may not lead a person to know Jesus, but you continue to plant seeds through friendship and God does the rest.

As a Christian writer and author, your books become another way you plant seeds of faith. Just as your life is a light of example for others, your writing shines God's light through inspiration, knowledge, and creativity.

A call to write is often birthed out of a desperate situation in which you needed hope. The lessons you learned along the way become your inspiration and give you the creative energy you need to be able to share the love of God in a new way.

The words you write may be the key to unlocking someone's understanding about their own situation. Your words may lead a reader one more step in the right direction, or give them their next breath of fresh air. Your book may be the bone marrow match to cure a reader's emotional disease, and bring them wellness in the next their season of life. The godly wisdom you share may provide the spiritual water they need to live another day. Your words may provide enough wisdom-assistance to pay the deficit of a neglected and defaulted circumstance.

So write.

Write, even if millions of people have access to the words, but only hundreds read it.

Write, even if writing bares your soul, and you're left alone and exposed.

Write, for your life was meant to bring the hope of Christ to those who know and read it.

And so, God provides *Our Written Lives of Hope* . . .

Out of His Treasure

Matthew 13:52
"Then said he unto them, Therefore every
scribe which is instructed unto the kingdom of heaven
is like unto a man that is an householder,
which bringeth forth out of his treasure things new and old."

Matthew 12:35
"A good man out of the good treasure of the heart
bringeth forth good things: and an evil man out of the
evil treasure bringeth forth evil things."

Matthew 6:20-23
"But lay up for yourselves treasures in heaven,
where neither moth nor rust doth corrupt,
and where thieves do not break through nor steal:
For where your treasure is, there will your heart be also."

Matthew 13:44
"Again, the kingdom of heaven is like unto treasure hid in a field;
the which when a man hath found, he hideth, and for joy thereof
goeth and selleth all that he hath, and buyeth that field.
Again, the kingdom of heaven is like unto a merchant man,
seeking goodly pearls: Who, when he had found one pearl of great
price, went and sold all that he had, and bought it."

Over time, a relationship with God buries a treasure chest of wisdom deep within the soul. Meditation on the Word of God rolls a grain of wisdom-sand over and over, until it produces a pearl. Precept upon precept, line upon line, the longer the intimate relationship with God, the more the treasure multiplies.

And scribes instructed in the kingdom of Heaven bring forth out of their treasure "things new and old."

The scribes of the Bible were learned writers, readers, leaders, and educators. They were holy men of God who spoke and wrote as the Holy Ghost moved on them (2 Peter 1:21).

From inkhorns, scrolls, clay tablets and stone, to the printing press, typewriters, computers and wireless keyboards—the writer's tools have certainly changed. We are no longer penning the Bible, but through our writing we are living out our faith in the Word made flesh (John 1:4).

As I compare my life to the lives of ancient writers, so much is different. Education, technology and culture provide opportunities like never before.

Ancient scribes painstakingly copied the Biblical texts. Every detail had to be perfect, or a scroll was unusable. They spent years copying one scroll. Their focus was on quality.

I save to "the cloud," use voice-to-text software, and write in my spare time. I have multiple copies of drafts, use spell check and type 70+ words per minute.

They were men who were walking by faith with no predecessors.

I'm a woman inspired by the Word of God, which they penned. As I read, God plants a seed of thought into my mind and spirit, a word of wisdom begins to grow, and eventually I birth a book that begins to take on a life of its own.

Times have changed, but much is still the same. No matter how different I am from them, as writers our passion remains the same: it's all about Him. Elohim. Jehovah. Yeshua. Jesus.

As Christian writers today, we dig into our treasure (our personal relationship with God) and write about Biblical principals within modern cultural contexts. We create a new setting for the old story. We understand current circumstances in the framework of timeless truth.

My Call to Write and Publish

Isaiah 52:7
"How beautiful upon the mountains are
the feet of him that bringeth good tidings, that publisheth peace;
that bringeth good tidings of good, that publisheth salvation;
that saith unto Zion, Thy God reigneth!"

I was ten years old the first time I considered writing a book. It was a fleeting thought, and I pushed it out of my head with: "That's too difficult!" I didn't have another thought of writing a book again until I was 19, though I journaled throughout my childhood.

One of my professors at Bible College told me I was an excellent writer and that I should think about writing more often. Shortly after that I began to pray about writing, and I asked God to provide a computer if He wanted me to write a book.

Later that year, a friend gave me an old desktop computer. "Wow," I thought, "I guess I need to start working on that book!" I didn't know how to start, so I just focused on my schoolwork and pushed the thought of writing aside once again.

After two and a half years as a theology major, I transferred to a secular university and started on a new degree, this time with a focus on writing. I began writing for my university's student-led newspaper, *The Inkwell*. Next, I interned at a well respected local magazine.

Despite all the progress I made in my education to become a writer, I had too much going on personally to write a book. I had a lot of hurt to heal from. From 2005 to 2008, I experienced the deepest struggles of my young adult life. My emotions were pretty much in shambles. I felt as if I were living in a spiritual wilderness. I was in a constant battle for survival—mentally, emotionally, physically, and relationally. My life was falling a part and crushing in on me. Everything I knew to be stable began to turn upside down, and I had to acknowledge some difficult truths about myself and get help.

Despite all of my personal struggles, I finished my bachelor's degree and moved back to Texas to start grad school. In my quest for clarity, I sought the face of God at Parkway Life Church in Lumberton, Texas where I experienced unconditional acceptance, and began my healing journey.

In 2009, a year into grad school, I took a job as a full-time writer for a newspaper in East Texas. I was the primary reporter for the weekly *Hardin County News* that year.

As I was working at the paper, I had a great time going to local events, talking with officials, interviewing community members and always being in the know. It kept me busy, and built my confidence in my writing and editing skills. My experience at the newspaper was the training I needed to eventually start my business.

Sometimes God has to tear us down to build us up according to His plan. In the midst of the journey He speaks to us in a way we will understand. Thankfully, God knew how to speak to me, and I heard the silent messages He spoke to my heart and mind.

One of the most significant words I heard from the Lord gave me the hope I needed to keep moving forward. It also paved the way for me to receive the call to publish. Here's what happened.

One night after church, I was driving home down a dark road. A large owl swooped to capture prey in the middle of the road and flew right into the path of my car's driver-side windshield. I hit the bird, which was about the size of a fat house-cat, and immediately my heart sank. I turned the car around and pulled over to check on the poor thing. As my bright headlights beamed into his eyes, he wobbled a little bit and looked up at me, seemingly confused.

It was then I heard the still, small voice of God speak to me. "You've been hit really hard, but you are going to fly again." At that very moment, the owl flew away. It was a sign from God—I was going to be okay.

A few weeks after my encounter with God and the owl, I was in Austin at a church conference. I met two ladies who spoke words of encouragement into my life and continued to add to my owl story.

The first lady said, "I don't know anything about your life, but I feel like you've been living in darkness for a long time. I want you to know that the light of God's sun is about to start shining in your life." The second lady did not hear what the first one said. After one of the services, she came up to me and said, "Brightness. Brightness. All I see is brightness."

These messages didn't make sense until I was driving home through the Piney Woods after the conference. I received another "owl confirmation" that God was leading me to better times. Perched on a road sign in the brightness of day was an owl, eyes wide open, looking right at me.

About a month later, the Holy Ghost spoke to my heart. The impression was clear, "I've given you everything you need to write and publish books." I knew God was calling me to write and publish the stories of people who had lived in darkness and overcome to live in the light. These stories would bring the hope of Christ to people in difficult situations.

The name of my business came next—Our Written Lives of Hope, OWL of Hope for short. The name was partially inspired by the history of Isle of Hope in the Savannah, Georgia area. Historically, Isle of Hope was known as a place where all races of people lived together in peace in the midst of treacherous times of slavery, war and other evils shrouding the Old South. It was a story that inspired me. I liked the way Isle of Hope and OWL of Hope sounded similar, so the name of my business came to be.

My "owl experience" and call to write and publish occurred during the time I was working for the local newspaper and in the middle of grad school. It was a busy year. When would I find the time to write a book? I knew I was using too much creative energy at the paper. I had to change careers if I was going to write for Jesus.

The Lord opened the door for a new job in a non-writing field and I relocated to the Fort Hood area in Central Texas.

It was while I was living in Harker Heights, Texas, that I began to look for the first story God would allow me the honor to write. It would be two years before He brought the story He chose as my first book.

After two layoffs and a move to Fort Polk, Louisiana for another job, God's timing kicked in. In July 2012, I began writing my first book: *Angel, The True Story of an Undeserved Chance*. It was the life story of a woman I met at church in Alexandria, Louisiana. Angel had an amazing testimony of deliverance, and I had a desire to write a book for the Lord.

God led us to start the project though we had barely met. Eleven months later, in June of 2013, we had the book in hand and I had officially established Our Written Lives of Hope, LLC. I later shortened the business name to Our Written Lives.

I completed *Called to Write, Chosen to Publish* in 2015. It is the 20th OWL book, and my second book to write. The business is growing all of the time. I'm working with several new authors, expanding my reach, and writing my third book.

I'm excited to see what the future holds, and I look forward to learning and sharing the God-stories of our generation—Our Written Lives "of hope."

Known and Read

2 Corinthians 3:2-3
"Ye are our epistle written in our hearts, known and read of all men: Forasmuch as ye are manifestly declared to be the epistle of Christ ministered by us, written not with ink, but with the Spirit of the living God; not in tables of stone, but in fleshy tables of the heart."

Time has spun our approach to communication in a full circle. In Bible days, believers were encouraged by the fact they were living epistles, known and read by all who knew them.

Now, 2000+ years later, I'm encouraging you to write about God's work in your life—to create an epistle (a written letter) to influence your world.

Your nextdoor neighbor might not be the one who reads what you write about your life; your reader may be someone on the other side of the world who follows you online. It doesn't matter who reads your life. your writing, or your book, as long as you are "known and read" for the glory of God.

A Legacy of Words

Isaiah 30:8
"Now go, write it before them in a table, and note it in a book, that it may be for the time to come for ever and ever..."

The words we write will outlive us if we capture them properly. When we take the time to create a document of worth, organized and well crafted, we can preserve and easily share our lives through writing. We can pass down a written legacy to our children and their children. We can share and celebrate the joy, the lessons learned, and the history of our lives.

We will connect with our readers as we write our stories, and as they read them. We, and they, are no longer alone as we share our lives through writing, even though we aren't there physically as they read.

I want to leave a written legacy that brings glory to God and the hope of Christ to people in our fallen world. What will the message of your legacy be?

A Good Matter

Psalm 45:1
"My heart is inditing [composing] a good matter . . .
My tongue is the pen of a ready [prepared] writer."

Proverbs 18:21
"Death and life are in the power of the tongue . . ."

My heart overflows with good news . . . My tongue is like the pen of an articulate scribe.

Are you ready to pen the words that flow out of your heart?

Just as the words we speak hold the power of life and death, so do the pens we hold in our hands and the keyboards on which we type our messages. We can bless others with spiritual life through the written word.

People write every day. Some are writing a book. Others are working in the writing and publishing industry in another capacity. People who don't even consider themselves writers are writing emails, blogs, texts, tweets and status updates every day.

What are you writing? Is it good news? Does it serve a purpose to better the world? Is it growing the Kingdom of God?

Let us strive to be ready writers—articulate scribes—to speak life into the lives of readers through the words we write.

> Job 33:3
> "My words shall be of the uprightness of my heart: and my lips shall utter knowledge clearly."

Spirit-Led Writing

1 Kings 19:11-12

"... And, behold, the LORD passed by, and a great and strong wind rent the mountains, and brake in pieces the rocks before the LORD; but the LORD was not in the wind: and after the wind an earthquake; but the LORD was not in the earthquake: and after the earthquake a fire; but the LORD was not in the fire: and after the fire, a still small voice."

I've met a couple of people who compared the stories God gives them to write to taking dictation, or, if they were speaking, to reading a teleprompter. They seem to be so sensitive to the Lord. It is as if the words they write or speak pour straight from Heaven through their vessel.

There have been a few times when I've "taken dictation," but my more common experience of the Holy Spirit leading my writing comes from studying and meditating on the Word of God.

God isn't always as obvious as I'd like Him to be. I have to be quiet to hear His still small voice speak. God is direct, however, through His Word. I find it interesting that I still have to be quiet and focus to hear His Word speak to my heart as I read and study the Bible, just like I do in order to hear His Spirit speak to my heart in my prayer times.

What does it take to hear the still small voice of God? Quiet reflection. What does it take to read and hear what God is saying in His Word? Quiet reflection.

We have to focus and become quiet to read the Word of God, to listen to God's voice, and to write as the Spirit leads. I'm thankful God chose writers to publish His Word. I'm thankful those writers were sensitive and quiet enough to hear His voice.

How quiet have you been today? Did you hear His voice? Did He give you any words to write today?

He is speaking. Take some time to listen and to read His Word.

Psalm 17:2
"Let my sentence come forth from thy presence . . ."

Writing From My Heart

Jeremiah 17:9
"The heart is deceitful above all things,
and desperately wicked: who can know it?"

Writing is my best form of communication. I love to write because I can think about what I want to say and how I want to say it, without just saying what I'm feeling or what first comes to mind. Writing helps curb the trouble that comes from speaking out of emotion.

But sometimes, I get myself into trouble writing as well. Have you ever written a long letter or email where you vented? It's the letter or email you should have deleted but sent it regardless.

I am guilty. I'm thinking of three particular situations: one in which I hand-carried a letter to someone; another which turned into an email war; and a third where I wrote several pages but ended up destroying the letter without giving it to the person. I learned sometimes it's better not to share everything I write!

My regretted words shot from my heart and pierced straight through someone else's. What I wrote was the truth; it certainly was my perception of the situation. The problem was it came from my human heart, a heart the Bible says is so deceitful and desperately wicked no one can know it (Jeremiah 17:9). I wrote from my heart, but disregarded how my words would impact others people's hearts.

Sometimes my heart deceives my mind. I feel what I perceive is the truth, but in reality it is only my emotions projected onto the person or situation in front of me. My heart is not always the best source of inspiration for writing.

At other times, I write from my heart and create a beautiful expression of human emotion. I've written poems and songs with such strong emotion attached that I personally cry and have goosebumps every time I read them. I've expressed my heartfelt love for family and friends with no regrets.

Good *can* come from writing with the heart.

But there's a difference in writing *with* the heart and writing *from* the heart. I don't want to write from my heart, with my heart being the source. I want to write as the Spirit of God leads me to write, with all my heart and my soul poured out before Him.

Who is Leading?

1 Corinthians 14:33
"For God is not the author of confusion, but of peace."

A previous mentor of mine advised me to consider every action I take and whether it is truly the Lord leading me or not. She said God leads gently like the Good Shepherd He is. He walks ahead, calls out, and the sheep hear His voice and follow. On the other hand, she said, the devil drives like a rough cowboy, shooing cattle from behind—driving them fast and hard with ropes and noise, dust and confusion.

Anytime we feel a strong intensity toward action, often accompanied by feelings of impending doom, it is probably not the Lord. When the Lord leads, His peace is always present. God does not invoke anxiety in our lives.

That being said, what spirit leads you as you write? Is it your human spirit, some other spirit, or the Holy Spirit?

There are a lot of great people out there who are writing good and helpful thoughts from their human spirit. Books and literature on humanitarianism, psychology, family and relationship issues, common sense and daily living all fall into the realm of writing from the human spirit. A lot of counselors and business leaders offer great human insight to successful living and survival within this harsh world. I enjoy reading what they write. I need their earthly wisdom. It's good stuff. It makes a difference in the world.

Along with practical wisdom, the human spirit can also lead us to write from a place of overcoming brokenness, hurt, and pain. I think of the memoirs I've read from Holocaust survivors. Their stories of survival are incredible, even if they are not based in faith. People go through terrible situations, and we need to be aware of what is happening in the world around us—no matter how difficult it may be to read. We need to know it is possible to survive, forgive and move forward, even through hell on earth.

We need the honest truth about life. With a victorious human spirit, we can write about overcoming brokenness and have a positive impact on the world. That is the good that comes from writing as the human spirit leads.

But what happens when some "other spirit" leads us as we write? The word "spirit" can seem undefined, creepy or spooky. I had a professor who encouraged our writing class to "sit down to breakfast" with fictional characters, to listen to the characters and to allow them to tell us their stories. It sounded too much like a séance for my liking. I'm not interested in hearing voices from an unknown place tell me stories, though I do believe it can happen.

I had a friend who told me about a vision she had of a murdered child who appeared to her and told her part of his story. She wanted to write the story for our fiction writing class. I believe there are "spirits" of all kinds out in the world looking for a listening ear. It's up to us what and who we choose to listen to.

Another way we can allow some "other spirit" to influence our writing is by writing from a spiritual journey or walk that isn't aligned with the Word of God. For instance, if we are operating out of bitterness, unforgiveness, hatred, prejudice, pride, selfishness, lust or covetousness, anger, rebellion, restlessness, or revenge, then we are writing under the influence of an ungodly spirit. Any destructive spirit, or way of life, that clashes with the Holy Spirit would fall under this classification.

If a person writes out of a destructive spirit, their writing can leave a reader feeling unmotivated, depressed, anxious, or spiritually worse than before they started reading. When destructive spirits lead a writer, readers will feel the emotions associated with the leading spirit.

"But it's just reading! It's entertainment," some may say. Still, allowing destructive spirits to plant thoughts in our minds, may allow for oppression or possession in the life of the writer or reader. It starts off deceptively innocent by first allowing the writer or reader to live vicariously in ungodly creative fantasy until they are comfortable with it. Later, the destructive spirits may transition into influencing a person's actions and choices.

But there is another Spirit that can lead our writing. Holy Spirit-led writing comes from a place of peace, healing and wholeness, and aligns with the Word of God. Spirit-led writing has a higher Kingdom-purpose, an eternal goal, which brings Jesus to the world and grows the fruit of the Spirit within us.

Jesus takes the mix of our human spirit and all those other spirits we deal with, and leads beyond the good of humanity into a place of power and deliverance, wisdom and a word fitly spoken in season. The Holy Spirit—Jesus, God manifest in the flesh, as He works in our lives—can lead us to write principled works that can make a difference in a person's earthly experience and eternal destination.

So, in conclusion, here are some questions to ask yourself before you consider publishing the work you are writing.

What do you want to bring to the world through your writing? What is the point? What is the lesson?

How will your words touch and influence lives? In what direction will your words lead?

Are you writing from a place of logic and common sense, or a place of confusion and looking for answers?

Will your writing inspire, or will it drag others down?

Before you are ready to think about publishing, take a big step back and ask yourself: what spirit is leading your writing? Is it your human spirit, some other spirit, or the Holy Spirit?

Writing to Heal

Proverbs 16:24
"Pleasant words are as an honeycomb,
sweet to the soul, and health to the bones."

Proverbs 12:18
"There is that speaketh like the piercings of a sword:
but the tongue of the wise is health."

Writing has always been therapeutic for me. I've kept journals since I was a child. They are all stashed in a suitcase I can easily grab come fire or hurricane. Journaling helps me sort through all my emotions, analyze situations, and make life-changing decisions. I've moved from a place of desperation and distress to a place of peace and contentment through writing.

I often meet people who tell me they have a desire to write their story. They want to find a larger purpose for the pain they have experienced. As I listen to these would-be authors talk, it's easy to tell where they are in their healing process. Some are ready to write and publish, and others are not.

Some potential authors worked through their pain long ago, healed and can talk calmly about their stories and all they went through. Others are anxious about writing their story, unsure how to start, tearful and still very much in pain and seeking to heal.

For some of the people who are still in pain, talking to me about the possibility of writing their story is the first time they've made an effort to outline what happened to them on paper. In these cases, I believe writing is a very therapeutic form of healing and should begin as a personal exploration of their story, with less focus on publishing.

Writing is a process of healing for the author. Even if you're not completely "healed" from your experience, write. It will help you to sort the chaos out.

Write your story, honestly.

Wait.

Pray.

Think about it.

Go back, read and rewrite.

Ask yourself, are you writing from a place of woundedness or from a place of healing and wholeness? Writing to heal is different from writing out of a place of healing.

Consider where you are. Put no pressure on yourself to publish; just write. Bare your soul: the good and the bad. Don't hold back as you write.

I'm sure you've heard the quote, "Hurt people hurt people." I recently heard that line followed by, "Healed people heal people."

Write to heal, and then, when you're healed, write and publish to help others heal. If you're hurting, and not yet healed, your words may be full of pain, resentment, and destruction. When you write from a place of health, your words are reflective and forgiving.

Pain is sacred. Experience is valuable. Writing is meaningful. But do we all need to share our stories with the world? Not necessarily. And even when we do share our stories with the world, we don't share every detail or every story. As we write we learn to respect ourselves, our pain, our vulnerabilities, and our triggers. We set boundaries to keep ourselves healthy.

Once we know our limitations, we can respect ourselves and our pain through our writing without causing additional stress. Once we have healed we can share our stories with the world.

Healed Enough to Publish

Luke 4:18-19
"The Spirit of the Lord is upon me, because he hath
anointed me to preach the gospel to the poor;
he hath sent me to heal the brokenhearted,
to preach deliverance to the captives,
and recovering of sight to the blind,
to set at liberty them that are bruised,
To preach the acceptable year of the Lord."

Writing is safe. Publishing is a risk. Are you ready to take the risk and share your story with the world? Publishing is a big step not to be taken lightly. You need to be sure you are ready and healed enough to share your story.

I talk to many people who want to bless the world by sharing the life lessons they have learned. They want to encourage others who may be in the same place they once were, to help shine a light on how to get out of difficult and dark places.

Books can help guide the way for others.

In some of the darkest times of my life, my only comfort was escaping my reality by opening a book. In particular, reading the Word of God helps me replace negative thoughts with positive ones and gives me an entirely new outlook on life. Other books, by inspirational Christian authors, have also helped me. They provide practical wisdom to navigate the storms of life.

We all have amazing stories and life lessons we can share, but we must be healed enough to publish. If we aren't healed enough, we can open ourselves up to even more pain and further delay our healing. Unrealistic publishing expectations can lead to disappointment and inflame old wounds, especially if your book is about a painful experience you endured. This particularly applies if you're hoping that by publishing your story you will receive recognition, affirmation, or a sense of acceptance that you did not receive in life.

Unlike sharing your story on a freely accessibly blog, print and digital publishing with the hope of making sales involves marketing and selling your story. Published authors are expected to be the face of their books in a very public way. If you aren't ready to verbally tell your story in a group setting, you're not ready to publish your book for sale.

I remember a bit of wisdom from a 12-step workbook. First, we must write our story and share it with someone safe. We talk to our safe person about how much of our story we want to share in the recovery group. We pray about it. If we feel any anxiety associated with sharing certain parts of our story, then it isn't the right time to share publicly. We share when we feel safe. Feeling safe is the number one consideration to know if you're healed enough to publish.

You ARE Ready to Write!

You may not be ready to publish, but you ARE ready to write! Don't bog yourself down with the stress of thinking of publishing or marketing. Just write. Write to heal. Write now. When it's time to publish, you will know.

When you are healed enough to publish, you will not view your book as an extension of yourself, or your "baby." When you are healed enough to publish, you will be open to editorial feedback, and be willing to make your book the best product it can be.

When you are healed enough to publish, you'll be ready to be the public face and voice of your story. When you are healed enough to publish, you will have strong enough boundaries to share your story fearlessly.

Job 19:23-24
"Oh that my words were now written! oh that they were printed in a book! That they were graven with an iron pen and lead in the rock for ever!"

To the Chief Musician

Ephesians 5:19-22
"Speaking to yourselves in psalms and hymns and spiritual songs,
singing and making melody in your heart to the Lord . . ."

The Psalms are my favorite scriptures to turn to for comfort. The Psalms reflect every emotion I experience in life and my walk with the Lord. There is a Psalm for every praise, every doubt, every victory, and every question mark in the human experience. The Psalms don't gloss over pain or rejection, fear or unbelief. They express the heart, cleansing it from whatever state it is in, and leading it into pure worship of the One True God.

For many of us, writing is a form of worship. God delivered us from so much, changed us, and gave us joy. He is our praise. He turns our mourning into dancing and our sorrow into joy (Psalm 30:11 and John 16:20).

God can transform our pain into joy and comfort for ourselves and the world. That is what He did when He gave

His life for us. He brought comfort to our souls through His pain. He turned His sorrow into our joy.

Everything in our lives is for one purpose—to worship God. Pour out what is in your heart, no matter what it is. Empty your heart and allow God to fill it with His love. Work through emotions and allow the Spirit free reign.

When the Chief Musician begins to make melody through us—the instrument—we produce beauty that brings Him glory. I once heard, it is not the piano who receives the honor, but the skilled master pianist. So it is with the Christian writer, poet and musician. Our minds and our work bring glory to the One we serve. We are the instrument. He is the Musician.

I am blessed with an earthly father who is a writer, songwriter, poet, and musician. My dad is my favorite (and most challenging) author to work with. I was honored to publish his first book, a book of poetry entitled *Patterns of Light,* released in 2014.

As I look through all of the books in the *Our Written Lives* collection, his book is the one I treasure the most. As I hold it and read it, I feel close to my father, and our Heavenly Father. I am grateful for the living legacy of faith Dad passed down into my hands.

The following is a song written by my father, pastor, and mentor, U.S. Army Chaplain J.S. Hartman (LTC) Retired. His life inspires me to write for our Lord and Savior, Jesus Christ. He often plays his dulcimer and sings this song for the hospice patients he ministers to. I hear his voice now in my heart and treasure it.

I Feel Your Pain
By J.S Hartman

The dark clouds obscure your sky; the wind blows so cold and strong.
Heart heavy, your head bowed down; down comes the rain.
I see through your darkest night: the sun shines, you'll be alright.
I'm with you in sun or rain, child, I feel your pain!

I know what's behind those tears that fall from your eyes like rain.
The heartache, the hurt, the fears, the guilt and the shame.
You think that you're all alone and nobody cares at all,
But My love has never changed, child, I'm still the same!

Remember the day I died, the day I was crucified?
My hands and My feet, My side, I hung there in shame.
And blood-drops fell all around, soaking the barren ground,
Like fresh fallen rain they came when I felt your pain!

I'm here now to see you through, just trust in My grace today.
I'll turn those dark skies to blue, those teardrops to praise.
My blood and My Spirit too, will comfort and cover you.
I love you, My child, I do, and I'll never change!

I'll walk every mile with you, child, call on My Name.
I'll never change. I'm still the same. I'll bear your pain.

A Good Scribe

2 Timothy 2:15
"Study to shew thyself approved unto God,
a workman that needeth not to be ashamed,
rightly dividing the word of truth."

For centuries, long before the printing press, scribes manually copied ancient Biblical texts. The process of hand-lettering a certifiable Torah took over a year. Exactly 304,805 words comprise Genesis through Deuteronomy.

You may wonder why it took so long to copy the Torah. Ancient Jewish scribes were held to the highest standards as they replicated manuscripts. Scribes had to memorize 4,000 different laws and principals, which they were to follow as they copied the Scriptures in order to preserve authenticity and accuracy. The duplicate must be exact, no errors, no ink droplets, no mistakes.

In his book *God Breathed, the Undeniable Power and Reliability of Scripture*, Josh McDowell describes the process a scribe took to produce a scroll. A scribe knew "that miscopying what God said could mean misreading, mispronouncing, or, worse, misinterpreting and misunderstanding what God wants his people to know about him and his ways" (McDowell, 129).

Scribes wrote from right to left, and wrote below the line, unlike how we write today—above the line. The meticulous process ensured proper reading and pronunciation. They had to perfectly copy each letter.

To certify a Torah, rabbis counted every letter and every word after a scribe completed copying the entire 72-foot scroll.

Matthew 5:18 NKJV
"For assuredly, I say to you, till heaven and earth pass away,
one jot or one tittle will by no means pass from the law till all is fulfilled."

The smallest letter in Hebrew is called a "jot." A "tittle" is a small line added to the top of some letters for decoration. At times, five tittles were added to the top of a letter; the five small lines were collectively called a crown.

God cares about the details. He cares about excellence and truth. Every jot and tittle matters. God's Word is forever settled in Heaven (Psalm 119:89).

Before a scribe wrote a word, he said it aloud. Each time he came upon a word for God—*Elohim*—or a name of God, the scribe would stop, set down his pen, wash his hands, and sanctify the ink. In another tradition, the scribe would not pen the word for God if they had just dipped their pen into the ink. They skipped the word and came back to make sure the name of God would not blot. A word meaning God, or a name of God, could not be blotted or smudged at all.

The awe, reverence and love ancient scribes held for the Word is what preserved it for us today. Though we are not scribes copying the Word by hand, as Christian writers we too must have the same awe, reverence and love for Scriptures they had. Through studying, we must ensure the words we write accurately portray the Word (2 Timothy 2:15). We must strive for excellence, and listen to those who come after us to verify our words—submitting to editors, pastors, teachers, and those who read to verify content.

It's my prayer that we all be open to listen to and obey the Lord, that we are skilled in our craft, and set apart to create an anointed work, that we are "ready writers" with the discipline needed to write when we feel like it and when we don't, and that we write with pure hearts (Psalm 45:1).

The information presented in this section came from Josh McDowell's book, *God Breathed, the Undeniable Power and Reliability of Scripture*. I had the pleasure of meeting Mr. McDowell in person as he spoke about ancient scribes and presented a few of the scrolls in his collection.

The Man with the Inkhorn

Ezekiel 9

"He cried also in mine ears with a loud voice, saying, 'Cause them that have charge over the city to draw near, even every man with his destroying weapon in his hand.' And, behold, six men came from the way of the higher gate, which lieth toward the north, and every man a slaughter weapon in his hand; and one man among them was clothed with linen, with a writer's inkhorn by his side: and they went in, and stood beside the brasen altar. And the glory of the God of Israel was gone up from the cherub, whereupon he was, to the threshold of the house. And he called to the man clothed with linen, which had the writer's inkhorn by his side; And the Lord said unto him, "Go through the midst of the city, through the midst of Jerusalem, and set a mark upon the foreheads of the men that sigh and that cry for all the abominations that be done in the midst thereof." And to the others he said in mine hearing, "Go ye after him through the city, and smite: let not your eye spare, neither have ye pity: Slay utterly old and young, both maids, and little children, and women: but come not near any man upon whom is the mark; and begin at my sanctuary. Then they began at the ancient men, which were before the house. And he said unto them, Defile the house, and fill the courts with the slain: go ye forth. And they went forth, and slew in the city. And it came to pass, while they were slaying them, and I was left, that I fell upon my face, and cried, and said, 'Ah Lord God! wilt thou destroy all the residue of Israel in thy pouring out of thy fury upon Jerusalem?' Then said he unto me, 'The iniquity of the house of Israel and Judah is exceeding great, and the land is full of blood, and the city full of perverseness: for they say, 'The Lord hath forsaken the earth, and the Lord seeth not.' And as for me also, mine eye shall not spare, neither will I have pity, but I will recompense their way upon their head.' And, behold, the man clothed with linen, which had the inkhorn by his side, reported the matter, saying, 'I have done as thou hast commanded me.'"

Ezekiel 9 paints a picture of gruesome judgment and justice for sin, yet we see the mercy of God sparing the righteous at the same time.

The salvation of righteous people in this passage came through one man—a called man—who came with the other men of the city. All were carrying weapons of destruction in their hands.

> "And God called to the man clothed with linen,
> which had the writer's inkhorn by his side..."

God gave the man with the inkhorn an instruction to write, to mark the righteous, and spare them from death. "Mark their foreheads," the Lord commanded. The man obeyed and then reported that he had completed all God told him to do.

The inkhorn is a powerful weapon—it destroyed judgment against true believers in Ezekiel 9. What is an inkhorn? It's a container, in Biblical times made of animal horn, used to carry ink. It was the inkwell of the ancient days.

The man in the passage was a scribe—a writer. He didn't appear as a man of war, but he responded to God's call along with others in charge of the city. His weapon was his inkhorn. In his hand was the power of the pen!

The written word holds power—power for good or power for evil. Power to save or power to destroy. Knowledge is power, and the best way to communicate knowledge is through writing.

In the Harry S. Truman Library, there is a miscellaneous historic document file. File Number 258 contains a transcript of a leaflet dropped from American planes over Japanese cities, warning civilians about the atomic bombs that would destroy the cities on August 6, 1945.

> America asks that you take immediate heed
> of what we say on this leaflet.
> We are in possession of the most destructive
> explosive ever devised by man . . .
> You should take steps now to cease military resistance.
> Otherwise, we shall resolutely employ this bomb and all our other
> superior weapons to promptly and forcefully end the war.
>
> EVACUATE YOUR CITIES.
> ATTENTION JAPANESE PEOPLE.
> EVACUATE YOUR CITIES.
> EVACUATE YOUR CITIES.

Another leaflet warned:

> ". . . Unfortunately, bombs have no eyes. So, in accordance with
> America's humanitarian policies, the American Air Force,
> which does not wish to injure innocent people, now gives
> you warning to evacuate the cities named and save your lives.
> America is not fighting the Japanese people . . .
> heed this warning and evacuate these cities immediately."

Japanese prisoners created the leaflets on a newspaper printing press. American pilots dropped over five million copies to warn citizens. Each paper showed pictures of American planes dropping bombs. Japanese writing explained what was going to happen.

Did the leaflet in File Number 258 ever reach the hands of the Japanese? If it did, where did they run? Where did they hide? How many escaped?

An estimated 140,000 people died after an American B-29 bombed Hiroshima. Three days later, another 80,000 more died when the U.S. bombed Nagasaki.

On September 2, 1945, Japanese officials signed formal documents of surrender.

Secretary of State James F. Byrnes credited the leaflets as helping to lead to the final Japanese surrender and the end of the war. In a dispatch sent from Washington, Byrnes thanked Air Force personnel and the Psychological Warfare department for their superb communication job.

The power to save and the power to destroy is in human hands. Human hands wrote the leaflet. Human hands piloted the plane that released the warning, and human hands released the atomic bombs on Hiroshima and Nagasaki.

War is unmerciful. Judgment is terrible. Can there be any saving grace? Some may argue that if one life was spared, five million leaflets were worth it.

The Bible is God's leaflet to humanity. With an estimated over six billion copies in print and online, and in multiple languages, how many souls will heed its warnings? If one soul is saved, six billion copies are worth it.

Your book may not spare a life or lead to eternal salvation, but maybe it will offer hope to someone. If your writing leads people to read the only Book that can lead them to salvation, the investment of time, energy, and work is worth it.

We are all facing something that is out to destroy us, either from within or from without. Is your reader facing divorce, death, unemployment, addiction, broken relationships, depression, anxiety, or a lack of direction? Has God called you, as the man with the inkhorn, to spare others through the power of writing?

Do not be dismayed if not everyone heeds the warnings. It is our job to write, and their job to choose.

The information presented in this section came from: Williams, Josette. (2009). Paths to Peace. *The Information War in the Pacific*, 1945. Accessed July 20, 2015, on CIA.gov. And from: *Leaflets warning Japanese of Atomic Bomb*, 1945. Accessed July 20, 2015 on PBS.org.

The Truthful Pen

Jeremiah 8:7-8 NIV
"My people do not know the requirements of the Lord. How can you say, 'We are wise, for we have the law of the Lord,' when actually the lying pen of the scribes has handled it falsely?'"

Verbal Integrity. It's a term I have rarely heard, but it stands out in my mind. If a person has verbal integrity, the words they speak are true. There is a wholeness, a full integration, between what they say, how they live, and what they know to be true. There are no fractures. The speaker is undivided.

As Christian writers, we must write with integrity. If we are called to write, we are called to not only write the truth, but to live it. God did not call us to glorify Him only through our writing, but through our lives and the way we live.

It doesn't matter what any other person says, we must align ourselves with the Word of God—the pure Truth—pick up our cross and follow Him.

There are many "lying pens" of the so-called wise and worldly people of today. We must come out from among them, be separate, holy, sanctified, filled with the Holy Ghost, and conduits of God's Spirit.

We begin on our knees. We find our inspiration in the Word. We come into a productive creative balance through prayer and worship. We seek our Lord's direction on what to write, how to live, and how to lead. Our writing submits to Truth. He is the Author and Finisher of our faith.

A powerful prayer life leads a Christian writer to have a powerful writing life. The intimacy that comes with faithfulness to prayer produces anointed writing. Spiritual disciplines train for commitment to writing.

The cleansing power of repentance and the infilling of the Holy Ghost rids us of sin's influence and opens our ears to hear God, our eyes to see Him, and our hearts to know Him. Jesus is the Way we follow, the Truth we know, and the Light by which we write.

Leviticus 11:44
"For I am the LORD your God: ye shall therefore sanctify yourselves, and ye shall be holy; for I am holy . . ."

2 Corinthians 6:16-17
"And what agreement hath the temple of God with idols? for ye are the temple of the living God; as God hath said, I will dwell in them, and walk in them; and I will be their God, and they shall be my people. Wherefore come out from among them, and be ye separate, saith the Lord, and touch not the unclean thing; and I will receive you."

Scribes and Pharisees

Luke 20:46-47
"Beware of the scribes, which desire to walk in long robes, and love greetings in the markets, and the highest seats in the synagogues, and the chief rooms at feasts; which devour widows' houses, and for a shew make long prayers . . ."

When we don't know how to start writing, we often seek out a person we know who has experienced success as a writer. If you have ever had a desire to write, it is likely you have reached out to someone you had confidence in, someone you considered an accomplished writer. I began my professional writing journey hoping to find a mentor. I wanted someone to lead and guide me through the process.

Teachers and writing classes were the most helpful when it came to learning the craft of writing. School, as well as working in the communication industry, trained me to produce completed work. I work well when I have a deadline.

I also joined a local writing group, which had a very positive impact on me. It was great way to get practical writing tips and encourage each other to meet writing goals.

Publishing was a different story. The people I knew who had published a book did not seem to know the worth of their experience, or at least they were not willing to share it. Authors I attempted to talk to snubbed me. I must not have been talking to the right people . . .

Instead of learning from experienced authors, I started researching various publishing options. Salesman began bombarding me with ads, phone calls, and expensive publishing packages. My interactions were mainly unhelpful.

I had similar experiences when it came to ministry. I acknowledged a call to Christian ministry and dedicated my life to the Lord at a young age, but when I reached out to people I respected who were actively involved in "ministry," more often than not, they pushed me away. I gave up looking for a ministry mentor and lost admiration for some people in church leadership because of the way they treated me. Even though I was doing everything "right," it wasn't enough for them to invest in me, or so it seemed. I couldn't live up to the expectations of these modern Pharisees.

I began to battle against low self-esteem. The enemy of my soul tempted me with lies after abusive spiritual leaders caused damage, members of higher academia devalued my work as a Christian writer, and traditional publishers would not speak to me. What I didn't realize was that the entire time, I had what it takes within me to be a minister, writer, and publisher. I didn't need the people I thought I needed. I needed Jesus, time, and experience.

When I was a child, I had a vision of who I would be as an adult. She was already within me; I just had to grow into her. I'm still growing, but I'm further along from where I started.

Now, I seek to help new Christian writers and authors. I want to extend to them the fellowship, mentorship, and acceptance I needed as I started my journey.

Christian writers, you are the reason why I'm writing *Called to Write, Chosen to Publish*. This book is my gift to you. I can't magically transfer my experience and knowledge to you, but I can offer mentorship and fellowship through writing and coaching.

And so, to you I say, "Beware of Scribes and Pharisees." Yes, they are still around. In the Bible, they were the leaders, the teachers of the law, the "perfect" ones. Today, Pharisees are the spiritually "perfect" among us. They study the law, and do all they can to live it out. They don't spend time with people who don't live up to their standards.

Today's Scribes have every "i" dotted and "t" crossed. Their grammar is perfect, and they are quick to point out when yours isn't. They devalue people who don't live up to their ideals of perfection. They know it all and are often credentialed to prove it. They allow no room for mistakes.

In ancient times, a perfectionist mentality was necessary for scribes to preserve the accuracy of scripture. Excellence and perfectionism are still valuable and important personal character traits needed in many careers—healthcare, counseling, editing, teaching, the military, and many other fields. We need accuracy, attention to detail, and commitment to giving our best.

Despite excellence being a positive trait at times, Jesus warned that the spirit of the Scribes and Pharisees—perfectionism—is destructive as way of life and treating others. As a new writer, it's important to write and not focus on the imperfections. Build your confidence and work on your craft. Find your voice, and don't let a Scribe or Pharisee cut you down before you have a chance to bloom.

Beware of Scribes and Pharisees. They nit-pick and must have it their way. They are perfectionists who demand, push and control. They are highly critical, and being around them can cause you to experience self-doubt and lose motivation for pursuing your dream to write and publish.

Jesus didn't hang out with Scribes and Pharisees as if they were best friends. He chose regular people, with a variety of personalities and imperfections. He spent time with real people. I have no doubt He would have spent just as much time with Scribes and Pharisees had they allowed Him, but they were not willing to be vessels of the Gospel, or admit imperfection or need.

I guarantee you will run into "Scribes and Pharisees" on your writing and publishing journey. As a new writer, watch out for them and steer clear. After a while of navigating the waters of the writing crowd, you will learn to avoid those who aren't good for you, and listen to those who are.

But then a new danger comes around. It's a very real temptation for experienced writers and publishers to fall into the "perfect" pattern and become a Scribe or Pharisee themselves. Guard your heart, especially as you learn, grow, and succeed. Remember who you are in Christ.

Not everyone is called to work with us. We are all called to work with different teams and people. If someone appears not to connect, there is a reason. Move on. Seek the Lord on your journey. Don't allow anyone to infect you with negativity, or to detour you from the path God put you on.

If you are called to write and chosen to publish, seek God, and He will bring it to pass.

Writing with Grace

2 Corinthians 12:9
"And he said unto me, My grace is sufficient for thee:
for my strength is made perfect in weakness.
Most gladly therefore will I rather glory in my infirmities,
that the power of Christ may rest upon me."

Grace. The dictionary provides several variations of the definition of grace.

- *Grace:* simple elegance or refinement of movement.
- *Grace:* the free and unmerited favor of God.
- *Grace:* to honor or credit someone or something by one's presence.
- *Grace:* a period officially allowed for the payment of a sum due, or for compliance with a law or condition, especially an extended period granted as a special favor.
- *Grace:* a short prayer of thanks said before a meal.
- *Grace:* used as a form of description or address for a duke, duchess, or archbishop.

Strong's Concordance and Greek Lexicon offers similar definitions for the way the word grace is used in the New Testament.

- *Grace:* to have compassion on; to pity; to show or obtain mercy.
- *Grace:* good suitableness, gracefulness.
- *Grace:* to be grateful, to express gratitude toward, to say grace at a meal.
- *Grace:* graciousness, the divine influence upon the heart and its reflection in the life.
- *Grace:* endue with special honor, to make accepted, to be highly favored.

When it comes to writing with grace, almost all of these definitions apply. Our writing should progress from one idea to the next, seamless like a skilled ballet dancer flowing gracefully with the music, or the message, of our work.

When we write with grace—the unmerited favor of God—we write with the Lord's blessing on our work. We walk in His power and authority, imperfect in our weakness, but strong in His favor and grace.

When we write with grace, we honor others by sharing our thoughts and insights with them. We honor what we have to offer by presenting our work professionally and in a way that glorifies God.

We write with grace when we give ourselves time to make things right. We give ourselves breathing room to make mistakes. We write the first draft, and we go back over it again and again, refining, clarifying, and making our writing as excellent as it can be.

We write with grace when we write with a spirit of thankfulness. We prepare our books as we prepare a meal, thoughtfully with consideration as to how it will feed and nourish our readers.

But writing and finishing a work isn't as simple as following a recipe. It may be frustrating. Our words may escape us, and we may be left staring at a blank screen. It may take months or years to complete our work. Write in that grace period.

Writing will take hours of hard, heart-wrenching concentration. We will find ourselves in weakness as we write, and in need of grace.

The writing process is messy, like life. But God's grace is sufficient. Let us, "therefore, glory in our infirmities that the power of Christ may rest on us" as we write with grace (2 Corinthians 12:9).

And, Behold, It Was Very Good

Genesis 1:31
"And God saw every thing that he had made,
and, behold, it was very good.
And the evening and the morning were the sixth day."

I tell the authors I work with to keep in mind what the professors say is true: "Writing is rewriting." Authors must be prepared to write and then rewrite their books at least three times. They will read or listen to their book read aloud six times before it is all over—sometimes alone, at other times with a friend. It's a tedious process, but it is the way to excellent completion.

Excellent completion—not perfection.

Even "best sellers" contain typos. "Scribes and Pharisees" pride themselves in finding mistakes as they read work by popular authors. But the truth is, we are all human and whatever humans do, the best we can hope for is goodness—not perfection.

When God created the world, it took Him six days. Then He took a step back and said, "It is very good."

He didn't say it was perfect. He didn't say there weren't issues. He didn't say it didn't need work, help, or a Savior. He said it was "very good." We all fall short of perfection, but we are also a "very good" creation.

The Biblical word picture used to describe sin is "to miss the mark," as if we were shooting an arrow at a target and missed. We will all miss the mark and fall short of the glory of God. Paul, the greatest writer of the New Testament, understood the concept of "missing the mark" of perfection. He wrote that our imperfections show Christ's perfection (2 Corinthians 12:9).

Knowing God has created me to be "very good" and not "perfect" helps me work with my mistakes and keep moving forward. In the words of Paul, though we miss the mark and fall short, we still "press toward the mark for the prize of the high calling of God in Christ Jesus" (Philippians 3:12-14).

As hard as we work to create a book, as much of our hearts and lives that we pour out into our writing, it will not be perfect.

But it can be very good.

And that is what we are aiming for.

Habakkuk 2:2
"And the Lord answered me, and said,
Write the vision, and make it plain upon tables..."

The Making of Many Books

Ecclesiastics 12:12
"And further, by these, my son, be admonished:
of making many books there is no end;
and much study is a weariness of the flesh."

We all have a story inside of us, and most of us have at least one book, if not more, that could come from our life. It is estimated that over 320 million people currently live in the United States. Even though we all have a book inside of us, not all of us are willing or able to write or share our stories, but quite a few of us are willing and able.

Over one million books published in 2013. Among them, over 18,000 were religious books. These statistics come from Bowker, the official U.S. ISBN Agency, and only include books registered with the agency. That means there are even more books published each year than we even know of.

There are a lot of books available and many of them have great content. What is different about your story? What sets it apart? What will make your book different?

Statistics show the average book sells less than 250 copies per year and less than 3,000 copies over its lifetime.

Publishing a book is probably not going to make you a millionaire, so if you're in it for the cash, rethink your commitment.

If it's not about the money, then keep pursuing your publishing goals! Most book sales occur when the author has a speaking ministry, or a business that puts them in front of a lot of people. They have a built-in community or following to sell to. It is possible to sell a lot of books if you're a go-getter who can set up a vendor table, if you travel and speak, if you love talking to people, and if you're not afraid to promote your book.

Most of the authors I work with have a desire to publish a book to complement their ministry or business. A book can be a tool to make lasting connections with people as supporters or clients.

I usually don't forget a story I've read, especially when it comes to stories about missionaries I've met, which are my favorite to read. I am more likely to support a missionary I feel an emotional connection with, than one that I know nothing of. Books are game-changers and can influence the direction of a person's life.

If God gave you a burden to write and a story to tell, go for it! If you aren't a great writer, find a ghostwriter, or do your best work and hand it over to a hired editor.

If you stay the course, your book will impact lives for Christ. It may be 250 lives, or it may be 2,500 or 250,000. The numbers don't matter when it's about Jesus.

All that matters is your obedience to His call. Obey and trust the Lord. He will do the rest. He has a purpose and a plan for your writing, even if it's a healing journey and developmental process for you personally.

Just as with every other ministry, success is not about how many people you reach. It's not about how many people come to hear you speak, or how many attend your church, or how many you win to God, or how many buy your book. It's about Jesus.

Will your book glorify God? Will it lead people to Truth? Will it give them an appetite for righteousness?

Will it matter to you how many people read your book? What will you do to tell people about your work?

Answer these questions with integrity, then go and write!

John 21:25
"And there are also many other things which Jesus did,
the which, if they should be written every one,
I suppose that even the world itself could not contain
the books that should be written."

The Author and Finisher of Our Faith

Hebrews 12:2
"Looking to Jesus the author and finisher of our faith . . ."

Jesus—our lives and work are all about Him.

As Christians called to write, I believe the first thought we ever have about writing comes from our Lord. To produce an anointed Spirit-led work, Jesus must be at the center from the beginning to the end.

He gives the ideas for the book. He inspires the words. He is the motive. He determines the outcome. He speaks to the hearts of the readers.

Hebrews 12:2 calls Jesus the "Author and Finisher" of our faith. To me, that means He writes the book of our faith, edits it, designs it, lays it out, publishes it, and does with it what He sees fit.

He needs no assistance. He is the source. Our faith story is wrapped up in His story. Our faith is all about His life, which He so lovingly gives to us.

Before we sit down to write we must first kneel to pray. We must allow the Author to step into our hearts and minds, whisper His wisdom to us, and surrender our ways to His.

A part of us will die in the process of writing—just as we die to our flesh to live in His Spirit. As we die out to ourselves, God raises us to new life—an abundant life we never knew was possible.

As we deny ourselves, pick up our cross, and press forward in our writing, our lives pour out new life. The books we write are entirely new creations—pointing back to Jesus.

Ephesians 3:20-21
"Now unto him that is able to do exceeding abundantly above all that we ask or think, according to the power that worketh in us, Unto him be glory in the church by Christ Jesus throughout all ages, world without end. Amen."

Scriptures for Writers

Frank Ball posted the following scriptures on the North Texas Christian Writers website ntchristianwriters.com. Ball adapted each scripture to fit a writer's situation. Used with permission.

Job 19:23–24
Oh that my words were written with an iron pen on a granite tablet so my story could be read forever.

Job 33:3
I write honestly from my heart, seeking to make the truth known.

Psalm 19:14
Let my concepts and writings be acceptable in your sight, O Lord, my strength and my redeemer.

Psalm 27:14
While waiting for the Lord, write. Be strong and take heart, and keep writing for the Lord.

Psalm 45:1
My heart overflows with a captivating theme, for my voice is the pen of a skillful writer.

Psalm 119:105
God's word is a lamp that lights my writing journey.

Psalm 127:1
If God is our helper when we write, the stories we build cannot be in vain.

Psalm 143:5
When I ponder what to write about, I remember the plights of my past and why I now give you praise. Then I reveal your glory by showing how you've worked in my life.

Proverbs 12:6
The words of deceivers shed innocent blood, but godly writing saves lives.

Proverbs 15:23
Writers rejoice when they can reach their audience with the right words at the right time.

Proverbs 16:24
Writing sprinkled with humor is wonderful medicine, for pleasant words are like honeycomb, sweet to the soul and healing to the bones.

Proverbs 16:3
Commit your writing to the Lord, and your message will touch people's hearts.

Proverbs 16:9
Writers would like to chart their entire journey to success, but God wants them to take the next right step.

Proverbs 22:29
Writers who develop excellent skills in their work will be admired by their peers and will earn the respect of those they don't know.

Proverbs 30:18
Without guidance, writers will fail, so blessed are those who carefully follow publishing guidelines.

Ecclesiastes 11:6
Sow your seeds in the morning and keep writing until dark, for then you may reap a great harvest.

Isaiah 30:8
Write your message in an article or a book so it may be an everlasting witness.

Isaiah 40:31
Writers who trust the Lord will find strength in him. They'll be like eagles with spread wings, soaring on the wind. They'll be like the runner who has the stamina to finish the race or the hiker who won't faint when the climbing gets tough.

Isaiah 55:11
When the Lord's message flows through my pen, it cannot be void of meaning but will always produce results, fulfilling his purpose. It cannot fail.

Jeremiah 15:16
In devouring your Word, my joy and delight comes from spreading your message, O God of Heaven's writers.

Jeremiah 23:28
Beyond fantasies and wishful thinking, let writers publish stories that let readers experience truth.

Jeremiah 29:11
The Lord says, "I know the great things I have in mind for your writing—plans for you to succeed, not fail—so anticipate the future with eager expectation."

Ezekiel 37:20
Publish the pieces you have written, so people can read them.

Joel 1:3
Write for your children so they can tell their children, so your stories may live from generation to generation.

Nahum 1:7
The Lord is good, a wonderful retreat when we suffer from writer's block. He recognizes those who seek him for guidance.

Habakkuk 2:2
Use plainly spoken words so people can easily read my message and run to tell others.

Matthew 5:14, 16
Like city lights on a hill that cannot be hidden, let your writing shine so people may read your words and glorify God in Heaven.

Matthew 13:52
Writers in the Kingdom of Heaven bring forth treasured stories that are familiar yet refreshingly new.

Matthew 19:29
Those who have sacrificed possessions, relationships, and pleasures so they can write stories about Christ working in their lives will receive a much greater benefit, as well as eternal life.

John 3:16
For God so loved the world that he gave his only son, so writers who believe in him and share their stories will not die but will lead others to eternal life.

John 7:38
Like a mighty river, words will flow from the mouth of those who believe in Christ.

Romans 8:18
You can be sure your present pain is nothing compared to the value of a finished manuscript when it is published.

Romans 8:28
Rejections, unreturned calls, and ignored book proposals will all work for good for writers who love God and seek to communicate a message that pleases him.

Romans 8:31
So what can you say about your writing efforts? If God is on your side, you cannot fail.

Romans 12:2
Don't let the world around you dictate how you write, but let God change the way you think. Then your stories will be what he wants—good, well pleasing, and complete.

1 Corinthians 1:27

God has chosen our meager writing skills to impact readers more than bestselling authors. He has chosen our small, insignificant words to change lives that were thought to be unchangeable.

1 Corinthians 2:12

Because we receive our inspiration from God, not the world, we are able to write about how he has blessed us.

1 Corinthians 13:1

If I write with human excellence and angelic might without truly caring about my audience, my message is little more than a noisy gong or clanging cymbal.

1 Corinthians 13:1

If I write with the skill of a bestselling author, but I do it without love, my book boasts of greatness without out any real merit.

2 Corinthians 3:18

As we focus on the Lord's presence and write for his glory, all who give themselves to the craft are changed into his image, rising from one publishing success to the next as the Holy Spirit keeps working in our lives.

Galatians 5:16
Please understand, if you listen to God's Spirit within, you will write to please him and to benefit others, not to satisfy your selfish desires.

Philippians 4:13
I can write anything if Christ will give me the ability and stamina.

Colossians 4:6
Be gracious with your stories, flavoring your message with that which will answer the hunger for God in everyone's heart.

1 Thessalonians 3:1
Pray for the publishing of God's message, so it will be honored among others as it has been in you.

1 Thessalonians 5:8
In every acceptance and rejection, give thanks in your writing efforts, because this is God will for you in Christ Jesus.

1 Timothy 4:12
Don't let people despise you as a novice, but be a faith example by seeking excellence in your writing.

James 2:14
What good is it, fellow believers, if you think you should write but fail to do the work? Can your belief alone get your book written?

1 Peter 3:15
Make good on your commitment to the Lord by preparing to share your experiences with those who might not understand how you have survived your struggles. Always be ready to reveal why you have hope in this tumultuous world.

1 Peter 4:12
My dear storytellers, don't be unduly alarmed by the fiery ordeals that come to test your writing ability, as if this were an abnormal experience.

1 Peter 5:6

Respecting God's ability above your own, humble yourselves, and God will cause your writing effort to prosper in due time.

Scripture Resources

The following scriptures were used throughout this book.

Genesis 1:31

"And God saw every thing that he had made, and, behold, it was very good. And the evening and the morning were the sixth day."

Leviticus 11:44

"For I *am* the LORD your God: ye shall therefore sanctify yourselves, and ye shall be holy; for I *am* holy . . ."

1 Kings 19:11-12

". . . And, behold, the LORD passed by, and a great and strong wind rent the mountains, and brake in pieces the rocks before the LORD; but the LORD was not in the wind: and after the wind an earthquake; but the LORD was not in the earthquake: and after the earthquake a fire; but the LORD was not in the fire: and after the fire, a still small voice."

Job 19:23-24

"Oh that my words were now written! oh that they were printed in a book! That they were graven with an iron pen and lead in the rock for ever!"

Job 33:3

"My words shall be of the uprightness of my heart: and my lips shall utter knowledge clearly."

Psalm 17:2

"Let my sentence come forth from thy presence . . ."

Psalm 45:1

"My heart is inditing [composing] a good matter . . . My tongue is the pen of a ready [prepared] writer."

Proverbs 12:18

"There is that speaketh like the piercings of a sword: but the tongue of the wise is health."

Proverbs 16:24

"Pleasant words are as an honeycomb, sweet to the soul, and health to the bones."

Proverbs 18:21

"Death and life are in the power of the tongue . . ."

Ecclesiastics 12:12

"And further, by these, my son, be admonished: of making many books *there is* no end; and much study *is* a weariness of the flesh."

Isaiah 30:8

"Now go, write it before them in a table, and note it in a book, that it may be for the time to come for ever and ever..."

Isaiah 52:7

"How beautiful upon the mountains are the feet of him that bringeth good tidings, that publisheth peace; that bringeth good tidings of good, that publisheth salvation; that saith unto Zion, Thy God reigneth!"

Jeremiah 8:7-8 NIV

"My people do not know the requirements of the Lord. How can you say, 'We are wise, for we have the law of the Lord,' when actually the lying pen of the scribes has handled it falsely?'"

Jeremiah 17:9

"The heart is deceitful above all things, and desperately wicked: who can know it?"

Habakkuk 2:2

"And the Lord answered me, and said, Write the vision, and make it plain upon tables . . ."

Matthew 5:18 NKJV

"For assuredly, I say to you, till heaven and earth pass away, one jot or one tittle will by no means pass from the law till all is fulfilled."

Matthew 6:20-23

"But lay up for yourselves treasures in heaven, where neither moth nor rust doth corrupt, and where thieves do not break through nor steal: For where your treasure is, there will your heart be also."

Matthew 12:35

"A good man out of the good treasure of the heart bringeth forth good things: and an evil man out of the evil treasure bringeth forth evil things."

Matthew 13:44

"Again, the kingdom of heaven is like unto treasure hid in a field; the which when a man hath found, he hideth, and for joy thereof goeth and selleth all that he hath, and buyeth that field. Again, the kingdom of heaven is like unto a merchant man, seeking goodly pearls: Who, when he had found one pearl of great price, went and sold all that he had, and bought it."

Matthew 13:52

"Then said he unto them, Therefore every scribe which is instructed unto the kingdom of heaven is like unto a man that is an householder, which bringeth forth out of his treasure things new and old."

Matthew 23:34 & 37

"Wherefore, behold, I send unto you prophets, and wise men, and scribes: and some of them ye shall kill and crucify; and some of them shall ye scourge in your synagogues, and persecute them from city to city . . . O Jerusalem, Jerusalem, thou that killest the prophets, and stonest them which are sent unto thee, how often would I have gathered thy children together, even as a hen gathereth her chickens under her wings, and ye would not!"

Luke 4:18-20

"The Spirit of the Lord is upon me, because he hath anointed me to preach the gospel to the poor; he hath sent me to heal the brokenhearted, to preach deliverance to the captives, and recovering of sight to the blind, to set at liberty them that are bruised, To preach the acceptable year of the Lord. And he closed the book, and he gave it again to the minister, and sat down. And the eyes of all them that were in the synagogue were fastened on him."

Luke 20:46-47

"Beware of the scribes, which desire to walk in long robes, and love greetings in the markets, and the highest seats in the synagogues, and the chief rooms at feasts; which devour widows' houses, and for a shew make long prayers . . ."

John 21:25

"And there are also many other things which Jesus did, the which, if they should be written every one, I suppose that even the world itself could not contain the books that should be written."

1 Corinthians 14:33

"For God is not the author of confusion, but of peace."

2 Corinthians 3:2-3

"Ye are our epistle written in our hearts, known and read of all men: Forasmuch as ye are manifestly declared to be the epistle of Christ ministered by us, written not with ink, but with the Spirit of the living God; not in tables of stone, but in fleshy tables of the heart."

2 Corinthians 6:16-17

"And what agreement hath the temple of God with idols? for ye are the temple of the living God; as God hath said, I will dwell in them, and walk in them; and I will be their God, and they shall be my people. Wherefore come out from among them, and be ye separate, saith the Lord, and touch not the unclean thing; and I will receive you."

2 Corinthians 12:9

"And he said unto me, My grace is sufficient for thee: for my strength is made perfect in weakness. Most gladly therefore will I rather glory in my infirmities, that the power of Christ may rest upon me."

Ephesians 3:20-21

"Now unto him that is able to do exceeding abundantly above all that we ask or think, according to the power that worketh in us, Unto him be glory in the church by Christ Jesus throughout all ages, world without end. Amen."

Ephesians 5:19-22

"Speaking to yourselves in psalms and hymns and spiritual songs, singing and making melody in your heart to the Lord."

2 Timothy 2:15

"Study to shew thyself approved unto God, a workman that needeth not to be ashamed, rightly dividing the word of truth."

Hebrews 12:2

"Looking to Jesus the author and finisher of our faith . . ."

About the Author

Rachael Kathleen Hartman is a writer and publisher with a love for God and a commitment to serve Christian writers. Her mission is to inspire others with the hope of Jesus Christ, and empower them to write and publish for the Kingdom of God.

She owns Our Written Lives, LLC, a Christian publishing company she started in 2013, and The Grammar Queen, an editorial consulting and writing services company she started in 2008.

She is the author of *Angel: The True Story of an Undeserved Chance, Called to Write Chosen to Publish*, and *Facing Myself: An Introspective Look at Cosmetic Surgery*. *Called to Write Chosen to Publish* was translated to Spanish in 2018 as *Llamada a Escribir, Elegida a Publicar.*

She is a certified Christian Life Coach specializing in coaching aspiring authors. She has a Master of Science degree in Human Services with a Specialization in Counseling from Capella University, and a Bachelor of Arts in Liberal Studies with a Minor in Writing from Armstrong Atlantic State University. She also spent two and half years as a theology major at Texas Bible College and Gateway College of Evangelism.

Other books by Rachael Kathleen Hartman:

RachaelKathleenHartman.com | OurWrittenLives.com

Our Written Lives
Christian Publishing
www.OurWrittenLives.com

www.ingramcontent.com/pod-product-compliance
Lightning Source LLC
Chambersburg PA
CBHW071745080526
44588CB00013B/2156